THE LOOK BOOK

by Jane Belk Moncure
illustrated by Lois Axeman
created by The Child's World

CHILDRENS PRESS, CHICAGO

Cover and Title Page
Designed by Dolores Hollister

Library of Congress Cataloging in Publication Data

Moncure, Jane Belk.
The look book.

(The Five senses)
Summary: Explains that eyes are for observing different colors and shapes and things that are big, small, near, and far.
1. Eye—Juvenile literature. 2. Vision—Juvenile literature. [1. Vision. 2. Eye]
I. Axeman, Lois, ill. II. Title. III. Series: Moncure, Jane Belk. Five senses.
QP475.7.M66 1982 152.1'4 82-4517
ISBN 0-516-03251-8 AACR2

THE LOOK BOOK

Eyes are for seeing
colors everywhere —
colored balloons at
a country fair,

a flower garden,

an Easter-egg tree,

and birthday cakes
in a bakery.

Eyes are for seeing
all kinds of shapes —
city shapes against the sky,

the shape of a sailboat
sailing by,

the shape of an airplane
flying high.

Eyes see big animals at the zoo —

an elephant,

a tall giraffe,

and a kangaroo.
(Look! There's a baby, too!)

Eyes see small things everywhere —
butterflies in the air,

grasshoppers
in the grass,

or even tiny ants
under a magnifying glass.

Eyes are for seeing
things very close —
snowflakes falling
on your nose,

or a ladybug
crawling on a rose.

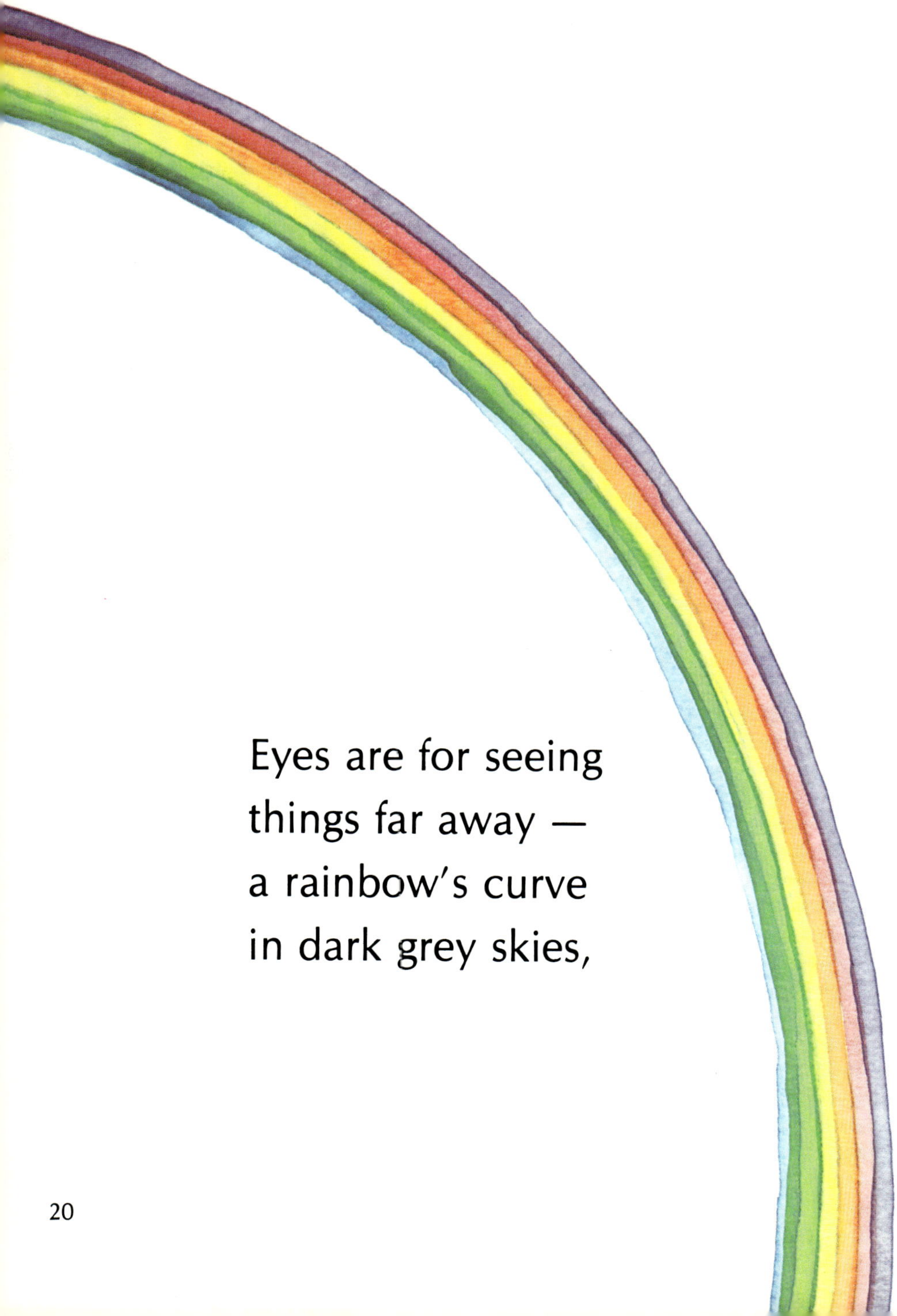

Eyes are for seeing
things far away —
a rainbow's curve
in dark grey skies,

or far far away,
the orange sunrise.

Eyes are for discovering . . .

a nest of bunnies
in the spring.

Eyes help you explore
places you have never been before.

Eyes help you
paint a picture,

tie a bow,

plant a garden,
row by row.

Eyes are for winking
when you're happy,

crying when you're sad,

blinking when you're sleepy,

twinkling when
you're glad.

Eyes are like
two magic cameras,
clicking pictures
of the world
around you.